A Celebration of the Life of

_____

_____

Born:

_____

Entered into Eternal Rest:

_____

" Love Lives On
The pain passes,
but the beauty
remains "

by Pierre Auguste Renoir

Guest Name

Thoughts & Memories

_____

_____

_____

_____

_____

_____

_____

_____

_____

_____

_____

_____

_____

_____

_____

_____

_____

Guest Name

Thoughts & Memories

_____

_____

_____

_____

_____

_____

_____

_____

_____

_____

_____

_____

_____

_____

_____

_____

_____

_____

Guest Name

Thoughts & Memories

_____

_____

_____

_____

_____

_____

_____

_____

_____

_____

_____

_____

_____

_____

_____

_____

_____

_____

_____

Guest Name

Thoughts & Memories

_____

_____

_____

_____

_____

Guest Name

Thoughts & Memories

_____

_____

_____

_____

_____

_____

_____

_____

_____

_____

_____

_____

_____

_____

_____

_____

_____

_____

_____

Guest Name

Thoughts & Memories

_____

_____

_____

_____

Guest Name

Thoughts & Memories

_____

_____

_____

_____

Guest Name

Thoughts & Memories

_____

_____

_____

_____

Guest Name

Thoughts & Memories

_____

_____

_____

_____

_____

_____

_____

_____

_____

_____

_____

_____

_____

_____

_____

_____

_____

Guest Name

Thoughts & Memories

_____

_____

_____

_____

Guest Name

Thoughts & Memories

_____

_____

_____

_____

_____

_____

_____

_____

_____

_____

_____

_____

_____

_____

_____

_____

_____

Guest Name

Thoughts & Memories

_____

_____

_____

_____

Guest Name

Thoughts & Memories

_____

_____

_____

_____

Guest Name

Thoughts & Memories

_____

_____

_____

_____

_____

_____

_____

_____

_____

_____

_____

_____

_____

_____

Guest Name

Thoughts & Memories

_____

_____

_____

_____

_____

_____

_____

_____

_____

_____

_____

_____

_____

_____

_____

_____

_____

Guest Name

Thoughts & Memories

_____

_____

_____

Guest Name

Thoughts & Memories

_____

_____

_____

_____

_____

_____

_____

_____

_____

_____

_____

_____

_____

_____

Guest Name

Thoughts & Memories

_____

_____

_____

_____

_____

_____

_____

_____

_____

_____

_____

_____

_____

_____

_____

_____

_____

_____

Guest Name

Thoughts & Memories

_____

_____

_____

_____

_____

_____

_____

_____

_____

_____

_____

_____

_____

_____

_____

_____

_____

Guest Name

Thoughts & Memories

_____

_____

_____

_____

_____

_____

_____

_____

_____

_____

_____

_____

_____

_____

_____

_____

Guest Name

Thoughts & Memories

Guest Name

Thoughts & Memories

_____

_____

_____

_____

_____

_____

_____

_____

_____

_____

_____

_____

_____

_____

_____

_____

Guest Name

Thoughts & Memories

_____

_____

_____

_____

_____

_____

_____

_____

_____

_____

_____

_____

_____

_____

_____

_____

_____

_____

Guest Name

Thoughts & Memories

_____

_____

_____

_____

Guest Name

Thoughts & Memories

Guest Name

Thoughts & Memories

_____

_____

_____

_____

_____

_____

_____

_____

_____

_____

_____

_____

_____

_____

_____

_____

Guest Name

Thoughts & Memories

_____

_____

_____

_____

_____

_____

_____

_____

_____

_____

_____

_____

_____

_____

_____

_____

_____

Guest Name

Thoughts & Memories

Guest Name

Thoughts & Memories

_____

_____

_____

_____

Guest Name

Thoughts & Memories

_____

_____

_____

_____

Guest Name

Thoughts & Memories

_____

_____

_____

_____

_____

Guest Name

Thoughts & Memories

Guest Name

Thoughts & Memories

_____

_____

_____

_____

Guest Name

Thoughts & Memories

_____

_____

_____

_____

Guest Name

Thoughts & Memories

_____

_____

_____

_____

_____

_____

_____

_____

_____

_____

_____

_____

_____

_____

_____

_____

_____

Guest Name

Thoughts & Memories

_____

_____

_____

_____

Guest Name

Thoughts & Memories

Guest Name

Thoughts & Memories

Guest Name

Thoughts & Memories

_____

_____

_____

_____

Guest Name

Thoughts & Memories

Guest Name

Thoughts & Memories

_____

_____

_____

_____

Guest Name

Thoughts & Memories

_____

_____

_____

_____

_____

_____

_____

_____

_____

_____

_____

_____

_____

_____

_____

_____

_____

Guest Name

Thoughts & Memories

Guest Name

Thoughts & Memories

Guest Name

Thoughts & Memories

Guest Name

Thoughts & Memories

_____

_____

_____

_____

_____

_____

_____

_____

_____

_____

_____

_____

_____

_____

Guest Name

Thoughts & Memories

_____

_____

_____

_____

_____

_____

_____

_____

_____

_____

_____

_____

_____

_____

_____

_____

_____

Guest Name

Thoughts & Memories

Guest Name
Thoughts & Memories

_____

_____

_____

_____

Guest Name

Thoughts & Memories

Guest Name

Thoughts & Memories

_____

_____

_____

_____

_____

_____

_____

_____

_____

_____

_____

_____

_____

_____

_____

_____

Guest Name

Thoughts & Memories

Guest Name

Thoughts & Memories

_____

_____

_____

_____

_____

_____

_____

_____

_____

_____

_____

_____

_____

_____

_____

_____

_____

_____

_____

_____

Guest Name

Thoughts & Memories

_____

_____

_____

_____

_____

_____

_____

_____

_____

_____

_____

_____

_____

_____

_____

_____

_____

_____

_____

_____

Guest Name

Thoughts & Memories

_____

_____

_____

_____

Guest Name

Thoughts & Memories

_____

_____

_____

_____

Guest Name

Thoughts & Memories

_____

_____

_____

_____

_____

_____

_____

_____

_____

_____

_____

_____

_____

_____

_____

_____

_____

Guest Name

Thoughts & Memories

Guest Name

Thoughts & Memories

_____

_____

_____

_____

_____

_____

_____

_____

_____

_____

_____

_____

_____

_____

_____

_____

_____

_____

_____

_____

Guest Name

Thoughts & Memories

Guest Name

Thoughts & Memories

_____

_____

_____

_____

_____

_____

_____

_____

_____

_____

_____

_____

_____

_____

_____

_____

Guest Name

Thoughts & Memories

_____

_____

_____

_____

Guest Name

Thoughts & Memories

_____

_____

_____

_____

_____

_____

_____

_____

_____

_____

_____

_____

_____

_____

_____

_____

_____

_____

_____

Guest Name

Thoughts & Memories

Guest Name

Thoughts & Memories

_____

_____

_____

_____

Guest Name

Thoughts & Memories

Guest Name

Thoughts & Memories

_____

_____

_____

_____

_____

_____

_____

_____

_____

_____

_____

_____

_____

_____

_____

_____

_____

_____

_____

Guest Name

Thoughts & Memories

Guest Name

Thoughts & Memories

_____

_____

_____

_____

_____

_____

_____

_____

_____

_____

_____

_____

_____

_____

_____

_____

_____

Guest Name

Thoughts & Memories

_____

_____

_____

_____

_____

_____

_____

_____

_____

_____

_____

_____

_____

_____

_____

_____

_____

_____

Guest Name

Thoughts & Memories

_____

_____

_____

_____

Guest Name

Thoughts & Memories

_____

_____

_____

_____

Guest Name

Thoughts & Memories

Guest Name
Thoughts & Memories

Guest Name

Thoughts & Memories

_____

_____

_____

_____

_____

_____

_____

_____

_____

_____

_____

_____

_____

Guest Name

Thoughts & Memories

_____

_____

_____

_____

Guest Name

Thoughts & Memories

Guest Name

Thoughts & Memories

Guest Name

Thoughts & Memories

_____

_____

_____

_____

_____

_____

_____

_____

_____

_____

_____

_____

_____

_____

_____

_____

_____

_____

Guest Name

Thoughts & Memories

_____

_____

_____

_____

Guest Name

Thoughts & Memories

_____

_____

_____

_____

_____

_____

_____

_____

_____

_____

_____

_____

_____

_____

_____

_____

_____

_____

_____

_____

Guest Name

Thoughts & Memories

Guest Name

Thoughts & Memories

_____

_____

_____

_____

Guest Name

Thoughts & Memories

Guest Name

Thoughts & Memories

Guest Name

Thoughts & Memories

_____

_____

_____

_____

_____
_____
_____
_____
_____
_____
_____
_____
_____
_____
_____
_____
_____

Guest Name

Thoughts & Memories

_____

_____

_____

_____

Guest Name

Thoughts & Memories

Guest Name

Thoughts & Memories

_____

_____

_____

_____

Guest Name

Thoughts & Memories

_____

_____

_____

_____

_____

_____

Guest Name

Thoughts & Memories

_____

_____

_____

_____

_____

_____

_____

_____

_____

_____

_____

_____

_____

_____

_____

_____

Guest Name

Thoughts & Memories

_____

_____

_____

_____

Guest Name

Thoughts & Memories

_____

_____

_____

_____

Guest Name

Thoughts & Memories

_____

_____

_____

_____

_____

_____

_____

_____

_____

_____

_____

_____

_____

_____

_____

_____

_____

Guest Name

Thoughts & Memories

_____

_____

_____

_____

Guest Name

Thoughts & Memories

Guest Name

Thoughts & Memories

_____

_____

_____

_____

Made in the USA
Monee, IL
29 August 2021